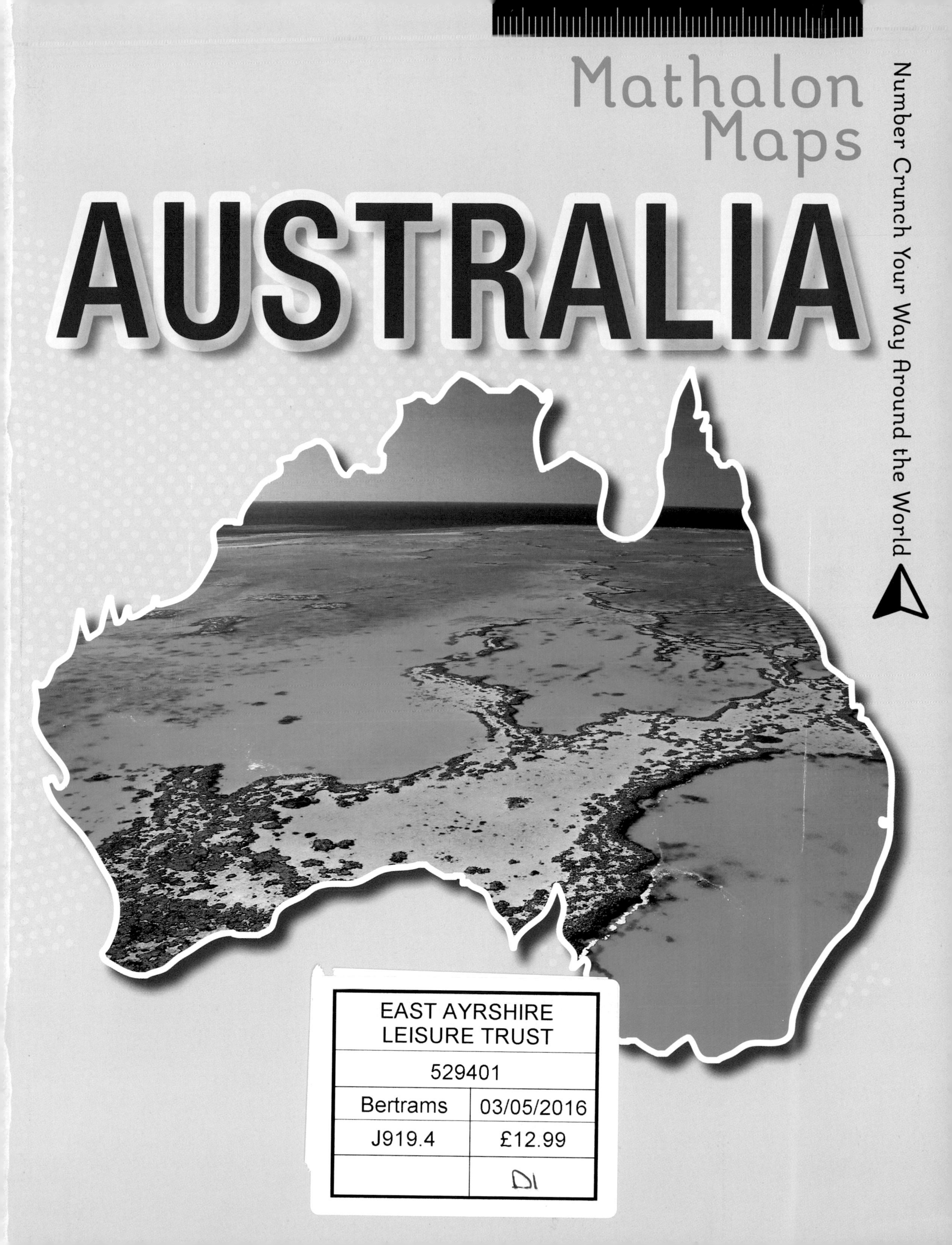
Mathalon Maps
AUSTRALIA
Number Crunch Your Way Around the World

Raintree is an imprint of Capstone Global Library Limited, a company incorporated in England and Wales having its registered office at 264 Banbury Road, Oxford OX2 7DY – Registered company number: 6695582

www.raintree.co.uk
myorders@raintree.co.uk

Produced for Raintree by Calcium
Edited by Sarah Eason and Katie Woolley
Designed by Paul Myerscough
Illustrations by Moloko88/Shutterstock
Picture research by Sarah Eason
Production by Victoria Fitzgerald
Originated by Capstone Global Library Ltd © 2016
Printed and bound in China

ISBN 978 1 4747 1594 2
19 18 17 16 15
10 9 8 7 6 5 4 3 2 1

British Library Cataloguing in Publication Data
A full catalogue record for this book is available from the British Library.

Acknowledgements
We would like to thank the following for permission to reproduce photographs: Dreamstime: Mogens Trolle 26l; Shutterstock: Richard J Ashcroft 14br, Attem 16c, Anton Balazh 7b, Baronb 16t, Ingvars Birznieks 15t, David Bostock 9b, Edmund Chai 23b, Curioso 17b, Dangdumrong 19tr, Larissa Dening 17c, EcoPrint 22c, Edella 15b, Susan Flashman 24l, Stanislav Fosenbauer 4c, 28-29c, GeorgeMPhotography 8t, Gevision 18t, 28-29b, Edward Haylan 5c, 29c, Ben Heys 21t, JC Photo 1, 11c, Anan Kaewkhammul 28l, Kwest 23t, Johan Larson 18b, Steve Lovegrove 25c, Robyn Mackenzie 19b, Christopher Meder 26r, Marcella Miriello 20c, N Mrtgh 12c, Masaki Norton 7t, Regien Paassen 27b, Pics by Nick 14bl, Production Perig 21b, Jordi Prat Puig 27t, Jason Patrick Ross 21c, Selfiy 4b, Vlad61 10c, Ashley Whitworth 5t, Ian Woolcock 24b, Worldswildlifewonders 6c, Peter Zaharov 13c, Jun Zhang 6b, Zstock 9t, 23c; Wikimedia Commons: David Iliff 13br.

Cover photographs reproduced with permission of: Shutterstock: Anan Kaewkhammul (top), Stanislav Fosenbauer (back cover), Selfiy (bottom).

Every effort has been made to contact copyright holders of material reproduced in this book. Any omissions will be rectified in subsequent printings if notice is given to the publisher.

Some words are shown in bold, **like this.** You can find out what they mean by looking in the glossary.

Contents

Australia

Welcome to Australia! This amazing continent is also an island, surrounded by the Pacific Ocean and the Indian Ocean. Are you ready to use your map and maths skills to explore the geography of Australia? Your maths exploration challenge starts now!

Indian Ocean

How to use this book

Look for the "Map-a-stat" and "Do the maths" features and complete the maths challenges. Then look at the answers on pages 28 and 29 to see if your calculations are correct.

Uluru

Lush and dry

The spectacular Great Barrier Reef is found on Australia's northeast coast. Also on the east coast is the beautiful city of Sydney, where the stunning Sydney Opera House is found. Australia's north has some lush rainforests, filled with many exotic birds and plants. The interior of Australia is mainly dry and flat, with much of it covered in a desert-like landscape called the outback, or the bush. There, the amazing, world-famous rock formation Uluru, or Ayers Rock, is found. Many animals live in the outback, too, including snakes, dingoes and wombats.

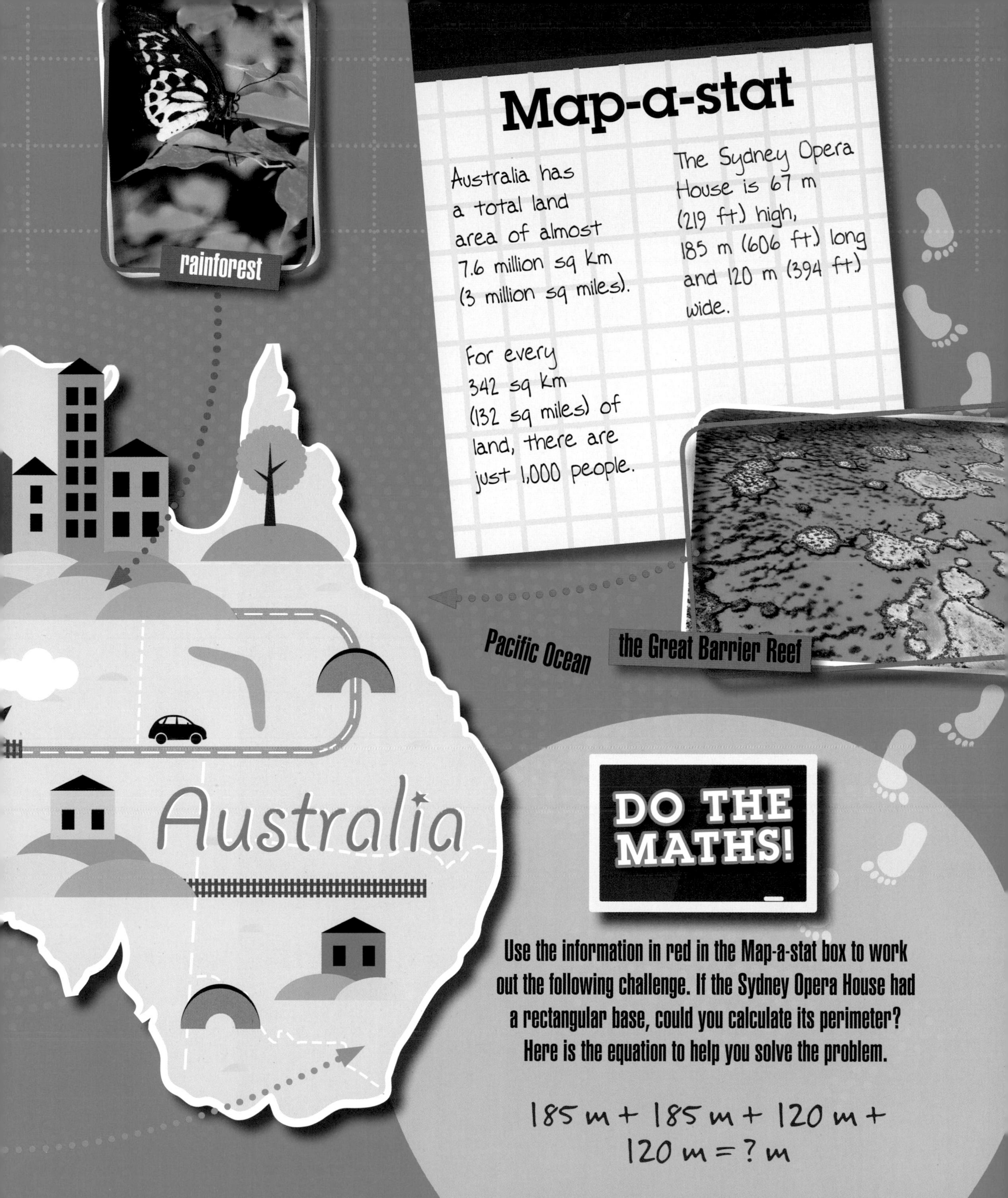

Map-a-stat

Australia has a total land area of almost 7.6 million sq km (3 million sq miles).

For every 342 sq km (132 sq miles) of land, there are just 1,000 people.

The Sydney Opera House is 67 m (219 ft) high, 185 m (606 ft) long and 120 m (394 ft) wide.

DO THE MATHS!

Use the information in red in the Map-a-stat box to work out the following challenge. If the Sydney Opera House had a rectangular base, could you calculate its perimeter? Here is the equation to help you solve the problem.

$$185\text{ m} + 185\text{ m} + 120\text{ m} + 120\text{ m} = ?\text{ m}$$

Complete the maths challenge, then turn to pages 28–29 to see if your calculation is correct!

World's smallest continent

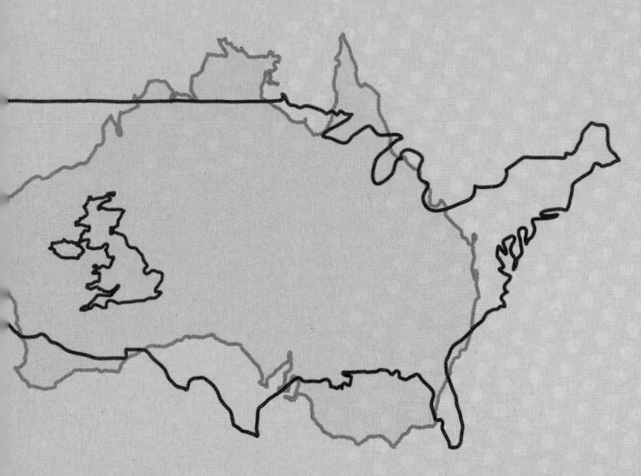

Australia is the sixth-largest country in the world, but it is the smallest continent. It is a little smaller than the main body of the United States, and 32 times larger than the United Kingdom.

Home sweet home

Aside from the mainland, there are thousands of islands in the oceans near Australia. Scientists call this region Oceania. Australia and its island **territories** have many different **habitats,** from deserts to rainforests. These habitats are home to thousands of plant and animal **species**, many of which are found nowhere else on Earth!

Koalas often come to mind when people think of Australia. These animals eat eucalyptus leaves.

Dingoes are one of the biggest predators in Australia. They live in deserts and **grasslands.**

Fraser Island is off the east coast of Australia.

Map-a-stat

At its widest points, Australia is almost the same length from north to south as it is from east to west. From north to south, it measures 3,859 km (2,398 miles), and from east to west it measures 3,999 km (2,485 miles).

As part of Australia, Fraser Island is the world's largest sand island. It has an area of 1,840 sq km (710 sq miles).

Australia's mainland is divided into five states and three territories. Tasmania makes a sixth state. Plus, there are six island territories and the Australian Antarctic Territory.

Australia is home to many kinds of **reptiles**, with 917 species.

Use the information in red in the Map-a-stat box to work out the following challenge. How many Australian states and territories are there altogether? Here is the equation to help you.

$5 + 3 + 1 + 6 + 1 = ?$ states and territories

Complete the maths challenge, then turn to pages 28–29 to see if your calculation is correct!

Tasmania

The coast with the most

Twelve Apostles, Victoria

As an island, Australia has a lot of coasts. Ocean water often brings a more temperate climate. This means that it is not as hot on the coast of Australia as it is further inland. It gets more rain, too. Because of this difference in climate, most Australians make their homes along the coast. If you look at the map of Australia below, you will notice that all the big cities and towns are found around the edges.

Australia's cities

The capital city in Australia is Canberra. It is a two-hour drive from the ocean, but it is still part of the coastal region. New South Wales, of which Sydney is the capital, is the region where Europeans first settled on the continent. Melbourne is the second-largest city, and the capital of Victoria. Rainy, warm Brisbane is the capital of Queensland. Perth, the capital of Western Australia, lies on the Swan River, and is a busy city. Adelaide is known for its churches.

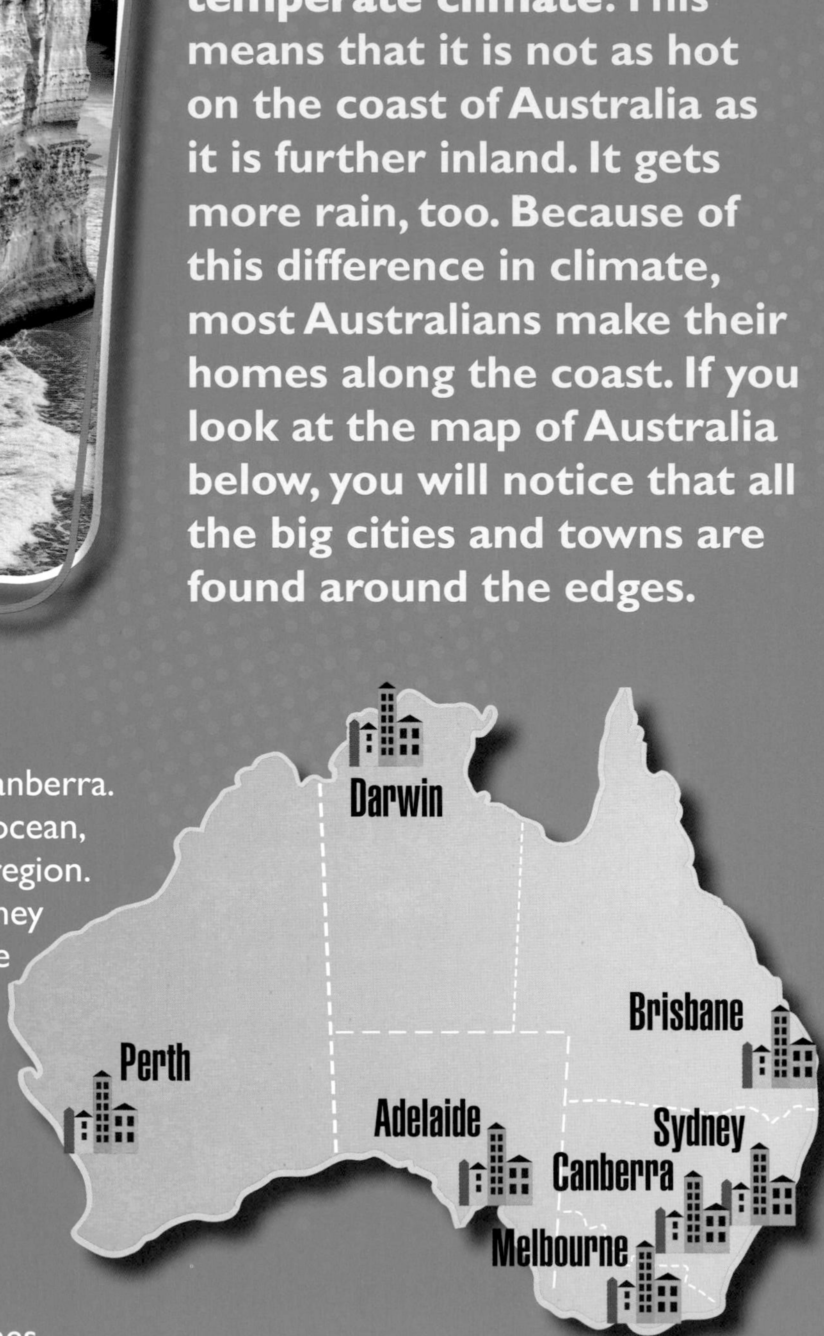

Darwin
Brisbane
Perth
Adelaide
Sydney
Canberra
Melbourne

Map-a-stat

The mainland of Australia has a coastline that stretches 36,735 km (22,826 miles).

All of Australia's many islands make up a total of 23,858 km (14,825 miles) of coastline. Kimberley is a region in Australia along the northwest coast. An area of the coast has a nickname, "the 80-mile (129-km) beach". Kimberley's coastline is 220 km (137 miles) long, and is home to a large number of shorebirds.

Queensland's Gold Coast

Brisbane, Australia's third-largest city, has a population of 2.13 million.

Use the information in red in the Map-a-stat box to work out the following challenge. How many hours would it take you to walk the coastline of Australia's mainland if you walked at a rate of 3 km per hour? Here is the equation to help you solve the problem.

36,735 km
÷ 3 km per hour
= ? hours

Complete the maths challenge, then turn to pages 28–29 to see if your calculation is correct!

The Great Barrier Reef

Great Barrier Reef

Australia

The world's biggest coral reef, the Great Barrier Reef, is found off the coast of Australia. This extraordinary structure stretches more than 2,011 km (1,250 miles) along the northeastern Australian coast.

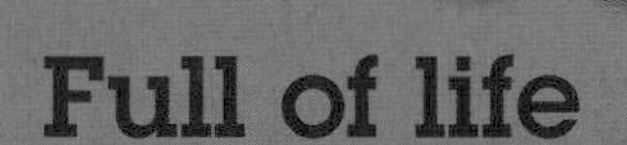

Full of life

The reef is home to many animals. It has more than 600 kinds of coral, 100 kinds of jellyfish, 3,000 varieties of shellfish, 500 species of worms, 133 varieties of sharks and rays, and more than 30 species of whales and dolphins. At least six species of sea turtles come to the reef to breed as well.

An incredible 215 species of birds, including 22 species of seabirds and 32 species of shorebirds, visit the reef or nest on its islands. The reef also houses at least 27,300 species of fish. That is 6 per cent of the world's total fish species!

Jellyfish and tropical fish are just some of the animals that live on the Great Barrier Reef.

Map-a-stat

The Great Barrier Reef is made up of more than 2,900 individual reefs.

The Great Barrier Reef has more than 900 islands.

The Great Barrier Reef is at least 2,011 km (1,250 miles) long.

The Great Barrier Reef is around the size of Texas.

The Great Barrier Reef is so large that it can even be seen from space!

DO THE MATHS!

Use the information in red in the Map-a-stat box to work out the following challenge. If you were to swim along the Great Barrier Reef at a rate of 1 km per hour, and back again to your starting point, how many hours would it take you to complete your journey? Here is the equation to help you solve the problem.

(2,011 km x 1 km per hour) x 2 = ? hours

Complete the maths challenge, then turn to pages 28–29 to see if your calculation is correct!

Mountains and highlands

Australia is the flattest and lowest continent in the world. Its average elevation is just 330 m (1,083 ft.) above sea level. That said, Australia is known for its beautiful, rocky outcroppings, such as Uluru. It also has a few highlands and mountains worth noting. Mount Kosciuszko is the tallest mountain on the mainland and is more than 2,228 km (7,310 ft.) tall.

Stirling Range National Park, Western Australia, is a bird sanctuary for species such as the short-billed black cockatoo and the western whipbird.

The Great Dividing Range

The Great Dividing Range, or Great Divide, is made up of **plateaus** and low mountains that run from Cape York Peninsula in Queensland to the Grampians, a mountain range in Victoria. The Great Dividing Range is 3,700 km (2,300 miles) long. Many of Australia's rivers start in the range.

Map-a-stat

Mount Kosciuszko is 2,228 m (7,310 ft.) tall. Compare this to Mount Everest, the tallest mountain in the world, which stands 8,850 m (29,035 ft.) tall.

Mount Townsend is Australia's second-tallest mountain at 2,214 m (7,266 ft.).

Uluru rises 348 m (1,142 ft.) above the surrounding **plains** and measures 9.4 km (5.8 miles) around its base.

the Snowy River, near Mount Kosciuszko

Use the information in red in the Map-a-stat box to work out the following challenge. How many times taller is Mount Everest than Mount Kosciuszko? You will need to round your answer. Here is the equation to help you solve the problem.

$$8{,}850 \text{ m} \div 2{,}228 \text{ m} = ? \text{ times taller}$$

Complete the maths challenge, then turn to pages 28–29 to see if your calculation is correct!

Three Sisters, Blue Mountains

Outback

Australia is the second-driest continent in the world, after Antarctica, where little rain falls. This means it is the driest continent that people live on. Around 80 per cent of the continent receives less than 6 cm (2.3 in) of rain each year. Much of Australia has few people and roads. This dry wilderness area is called the outback.

Deserts

There are 10 deserts in Australia. Few people live in these areas, though **Aboriginal** groups make their homes there. They have found ingenious ways to survive in the desert, including setting fire to the bush to encourage new plants, and therefore food, to grow. Despite the tough conditions in the Australian desert, plenty of plants and animals make their home there, too.

kangaroo

The Devils Marbles, or Karlu Karlu, were shaped by natural forces.

Map-a-stat

Only 3 per cent of Australia's population lives in the desert. These people include Aborigines.

Around 460,000 Aborigines live in Australia. There are about 500 different groups of Aborigines.

More **mammals** have become **extinct** in Australia in the last 400 years than any other continent in the world. In fact, one-third of all the world's extinct mammals were Australian.

According to the International Union for Conservation of Nature (IUCN) Red List, Australia has 10 mammal, 4 bird, 13 fish, 7 reptile and 15 **amphibian** species that are critically endangered, or almost extinct.

Sturt's Desert Pea is one of Australia's best-known wildflowers.

Use the information in red in the Map-a-stat box to work out the following challenge. Add up the different species that are critically endangered in Australia. Here is the equation to help you solve the problem.

$$10 + 4 + 13 + 7 + 15$$
$$= ? \text{ species}$$

Complete the maths challenge, then turn to pages 28–29 to see if your calculation is correct!

Australia's outback is home to a colony of wild camels.

Farmland

Despite the country's dry conditions, agriculture is an important industry in Australia. Australian farmers grow crops. They also raise cattle for milk and meat, and sheep for milk, meat and wool. Australia's land is most fertile along the coasts and in Tasmania. The grasslands of the interior lowlands are used for grazing. With irrigation, less fertile land can still be farmed though it is challenging.

sheep

grasslands in Western Australia

Farms and food

Much of Australia's coastal areas can get up to 32 cm (12.5 in) of rain each year. This allows many kinds of crops to be grown and provides rich pasture for dairy farms. The major agricultural products in Australia, in order of value, are cattle, wheat, dairy, vegetables, fruit, nuts and lamb meat and wool.

carrots

The Yarra Valley, in Victoria, is well-suited for growing grapes and producing wine.

Map-a-stat

Australia has more than 134,000 farms that cover around half of the continent.

There is a measure in South Australia called Goyder's Line, which marks the end of land suitable for crop growing. Land south of the line gets more than 30 cm (12 in) of rain each year, while land north of the line does not.

Only about 1 per cent of Australia's farms use irrigation to water crops.

Each Australian farmer produces enough food to feed 600 people.

Use the information in red in the Map-a-stat box to work out the following challenge. If each Australian farmer feeds 600 people, and only 150 of those people live in Australia, how many people is each farmer feeding outside Australia? Here is the equation to help you solve the problem.

600 people − 150 people
= ? people

Complete the maths challenge, then turn to pages 28–29 to see if your calculation is correct!

Eastern temperate forests

Springbrook National Park, Queensland

Australia has about 1,250,000 sq km (482,630 sq miles) of forests. Most of these are native forests, but a small number of them are plantations where the wood is used for lumber and other wood products.

Eucalyptus trees

When you think about Australia's forests, you probably picture eucalyptus trees. They are home to one of Australia's most famous animals, the koala. Eucalyptus trees make up much of Australia's forests and are **adapted** to the dry climate of the country. They are also adapted to regrow after fires, which are very common on the continent. People use the lumber, oils and honey made by bees that visit the trees. Aborigines also make many products, including dishes, musical instruments and canoes, using the wood from the trees.

Orange-thighed tree frogs live in some of the native forests in Queensland.

Map-a-stat

75 per cent of Australia's forests is eucalyptus trees. Much of the remaining forests is acacia and melaleuca trees.

There are around 800 different species of eucalyptus in Australia's forests.

Australia's forests are broken into eight types, based on the kind of tree that is most prominent.

Rainforests make up 3 per cent of Australia's total forested areas.

There are 2,212 species of animals classified as **vertebrates** and 16,836 **non-vascular** plant species in the forests of Australia.

koala

Use the information in red in the Map-a-stat box to work out the following challenge. How many times more species of non-vascular plants are there than vertebrate animals living in the forests of Australia? You will need to round your answer. Here is the equation to help you solve the problem.

16,836 plants ÷ 2,212 animals = ? times more plant species

Complete the maths challenge, then turn to pages 28–29 to see if your calculation is correct!

temperate rainforest, Victoria

Australia's rivers

There are 208 major rivers in Western Australia. The largest and best-known river system is the Murray–Darling River Basin. This system is made up of two main rivers and many **tributaries**. The land surrounding these rivers makes up two-thirds of the continent's irrigated farmland.

Sugarcane farms in Australia are often found near rivers.

Lake Cave is a beautiful underground lake in Western Australia.

A unique river

The Gascoyne River is 834 km (518 miles) long. It is unique because for two-thirds of the year, you cannot see it! It is what Australians call an "upside down" river, which means for much of the year this river flows under the ground. It flows above ground for only about 120 days each year.

Map-a-stat

Australia's longest river is the Murray River, which is 2,507 km (1,558 miles) long.

The second-longest is the Darling River at 1,545 km (960 miles).

The Murray-Darling Basin contains around 30,000 **wetlands**.

At its widest point, the Murray-Darling Basin is 1,250 km (777 miles) across and 1,364 km (848 miles) from north to south.

mouth of the Hopkins River, Victoria

Melbourne, the capital of Victoria, sits on the Yarra River.

DO THE MATHS!

Use the information in red in the Map-a-stat box to work out the following challenge. If you paddled down the Murray River at a rate of 3 km per hour, roughly how long would it take you to reach the mouth of the river? You will need to round your answer. Here is the equation to help you solve the problem.

$$2{,}507 \text{ km} \div 3 \text{ km per hour} = ? \text{ hours}$$

Complete the maths challenge, then turn to pages 28–29 to see if your calculation is correct!

Australia's states and territories

Australia has 6 states and 10 territories. The states are New South Wales, Queensland, South Australia, Tasmania, Victoria and Western Australia. Each state has its own constitution and government. Canberra, the country's national capital, is part of the Australian Capital Territory. Jervis Bay Territory and the Northern Territory are the other territories on the mainland.

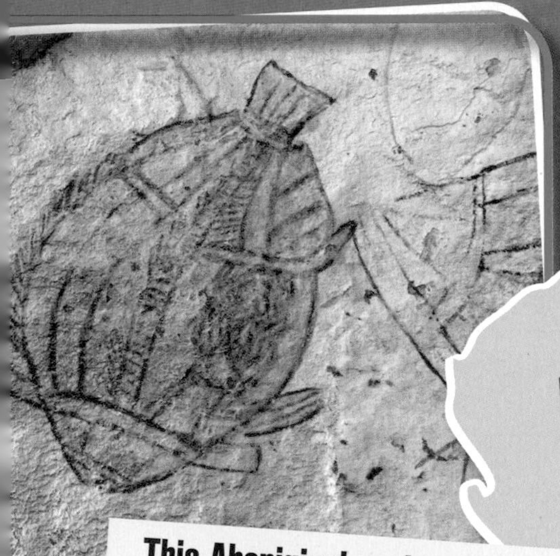

This Aboriginal rock art shows a fish painted in Kakadu Park in the Northern Territory.

Big and small

New South Wales is the state with the largest number of people living in it, while Tasmania has the fewest. The state of Western Australia has the largest area. It is 2,529,886 sq km (976,790 sq miles). Few people live there, though. Of its 2.5 million people, most of them live in the southwest corner, near the coast.

Map-a-stat

New South Wales is the most populated state with a population of 7.5 million people. Tasmania has the smallest population of the six states, at 514,700.

It is 1,198 km (745 miles) by road from Brisbane, the capital of Queensland, to Canberra. From Canberra to Melbourne is another 665 km (413 miles).

Central Australian bush country

Queensland is known for its coastal living and surfing.

This is the Sydney Opera House in Sydney, the capital of New South Wales.

DO THE MATHS!

Use the information in red in the Map-a-stat box to work out the following challenge. By road, how many km is it from Brisbane to Melbourne, via Canberra? Here is the equation to help you solve the problem.

$$1{,}198 \text{ km} + 665 \text{ km} = ? \text{ km}$$

Complete the maths challenge, then turn to pages 28–29 to see if your calculation is correct!

Tasmania

Tasmania is 241 km (150 miles) south of Australia. It is the smallest state by area and has the smallest population of any state, too. It is known as the "natural state" because it has so much unspoiled wilderness. In fact, much of Tasmania's land is **protected**, which means it cannot be developed or changed. There are 19 pieces of land that are **reserved** as national parks.

Tasmanian industry

Tasmania's main industries are mining (especially copper, zinc, tin and iron), agriculture, forestry and tourism. Because there is such a large area of wilderness to explore, many tourists come to enjoy the natural beauty of Tasmania. The state has many hotels, two casinos and several events that draw visitors, as well.

Tasmanian lavender

The Tasmanian devil is found only on Tasmania.

mainland Australia

Tasmania

Map-a-stat

Tasmania's highest point is Mount Ossa, which stands 1,617 m (5,305 ft) high.

The Tarkine in Tasmania is Australia's largest temperate rainforest. It covers 3,700 sq km (1,429 sq miles).

The Tarkine gets up to 240 cm (94 in) of rain a year. In the Pacific United States, the temperate rainforests there tend to get around 305 cm (120 in) per year

Hobart is the biggest city in Tasmania.

DO THE MATHS!

Use the information in red in the Map-a-stat box to work out the following challenge. How many more cm of rainfall do US temperate rainforests get than the Tarkine? Here is the equation to help you solve the problem.

305 cm − 240 cm = ? cm

Complete the maths challenge, then turn to pages 28–29 to see if your calculation is correct!

A land of extremes

Australia is a land of extremes. It is the smallest and lowest continent. It is the driest inhabited continent, as well. Australia is also famous for its dangerous animals. The saltwater crocodile makes its home in Australia and, at an average of 5 m (17 ft.), is the largest crocodile in the world.

saltwater crocodile

Tathra, New South Wales, offers a beautiful sunrise.

"The Land Down Under"

Australia has huge cattle farms, and grows many vegetables, too. It has **modern** cities and vast areas of unsettled outback. It is a beautiful place and its wilderness areas bring people from other continents, who want to see "The Land Down Under" for themselves.

Map-a-stat

Australia is one of the world's leading **exporters** of coal. It exports more than 301 million metric tons (296 million tons)! Australia also has some diamond mines.

While English is the main language spoken in Australia, more than 200 languages are spoken there, including 50 Aboriginal languages.

Australia's lowest point is Lake Eyre at 15 m (49 ft) below sea level.

Around 85 per cent of Australia's population lives within 50 km (31 miles) of the coast.

The world's largest cattle station is in South Australia. It is 23,677 sq km (9,142 sq miles), which is larger than Wales!

These beach houses are landmarks of Brighton Beach in Melbourne.

Aborigine

Use the information in red in the Map-a-stat box to work out the following challenge. If 50 Aboriginal languages are spoken in Australia, and 200 languages are spoken in all, how many non-Aboriginal languages are spoken there? Here is the equation to help you solve the problem.

200 languages – 50 languages = ? languages

Complete the maths challenge, then turn to pages 28–29 to see if your calculation is correct!

Maths challenge answers

You have made it through the mathalon! How did your maths skills measure up? Check your answers below.

Page 5

185 m + 185 m + 120 m + 120 m = 610 m

Page 7

5 + 3 + 1 + 6 + 1 = 16 states and territories

Page 9

36,735 km ÷ 3 km per hour = 12,245 hours

Page 11

(2,011 km x 1 km per hour) x 2 = 4,022 hours

Page 13

8,850 m ÷ 2,228 m = 4 times taller

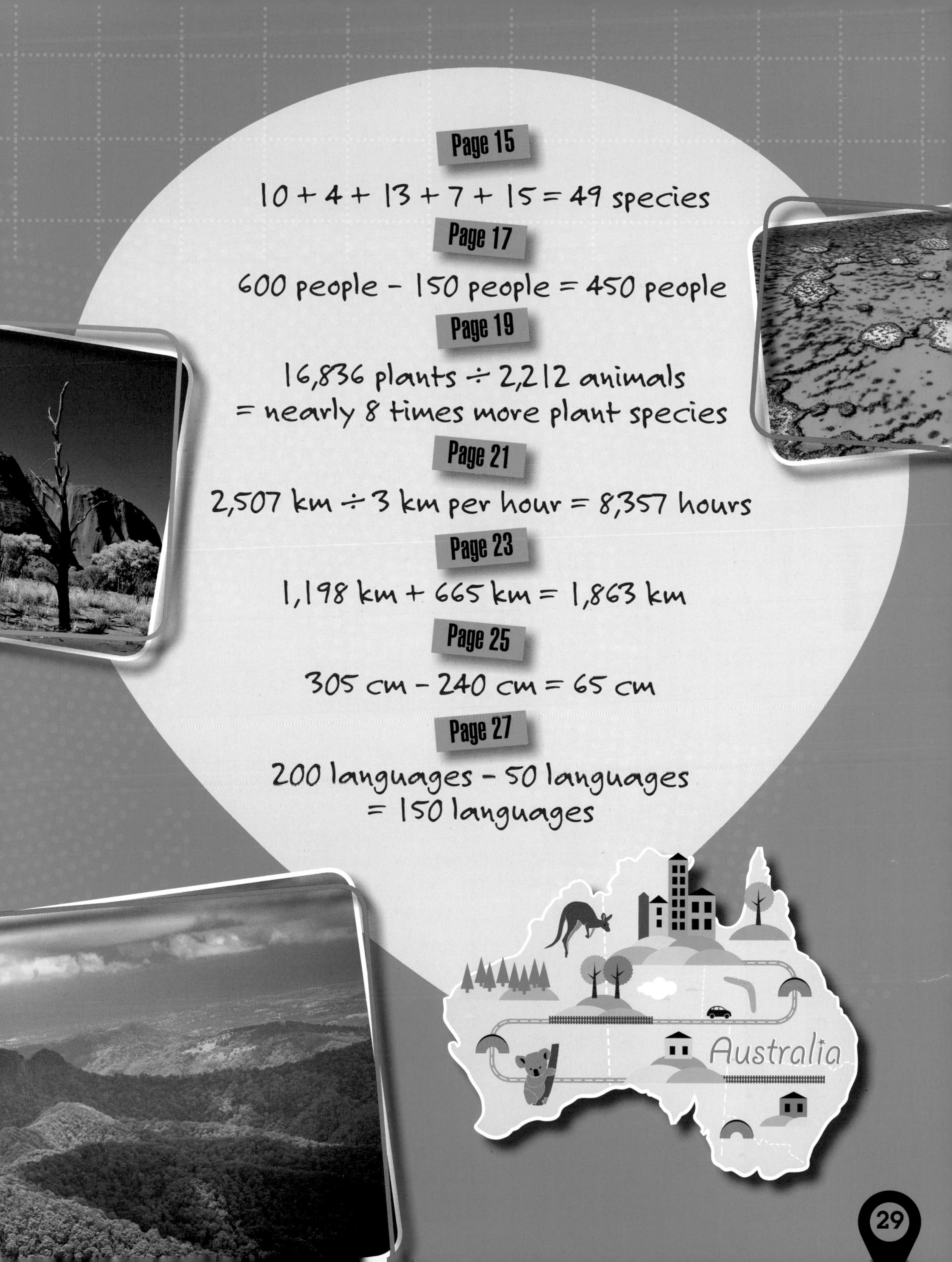

Page 15

10 + 4 + 13 + 7 + 15 = 49 species

Page 17

600 people − 150 people = 450 people

Page 19

16,836 plants ÷ 2,212 animals
= nearly 8 times more plant species

Page 21

2,507 km ÷ 3 km per hour = 8,357 hours

Page 23

1,198 km + 665 km = 1,863 km

Page 25

305 cm − 240 cm = 65 cm

Page 27

200 languages − 50 languages
= 150 languages

Glossary

Aboriginal relating to first people to live in Australia

adapted changed in order to survive

amphibian cold-blooded animal that spends part of its life in water and part on land

constitution basic rules by which a country or a state is governed

continent one of Earth's seven large landmasses

coral reef underwater ridge of coral, which is made from the remains of tiny sea creatures. Coral reefs provide a rich habitat for plants and animals.

dingo wild dog that lives in Australia

elevation height above sea level of an object or area

exotic unusual, not often seen

exporter country or person that sell goods to other countries

extinct no longer existing

extreme going past the expected or common. Extreme weather might be very hot or very cold.

fertile describes ground that is rich and able to produce crops and other plants

geography study of Earth's weather, land, countries, people and businesses

grassland large area of land covered by grass

habitat surroundings where animals or plants naturally live

irrigation system of watering farmland

lumber wood from trees that have been cut down

mammal animal that has warm blood and often fur. Most mammals give birth to live young and feed their babies with milk from their bodies.

modern using the most up-to-date ideas or ways of doing things

native forest forest made up of trees that come from an area or country, rather than those brought into an area or country

non-vascular not having a vascular system, which is a series of veins that transport fluid around the body

plain large, flat area of land often covered in grasses

plantation large area on which forests are grown for products, such as rubber and lumber

plateau large, flat area that is at a higher altitude than the surrounding region

protected kept from harm

reptile animal that has scales covering its body and that uses the sun to control its body temperature

reserved set aside as a protected habitat for wildlife

species single kind of living thing. All people are one species.

temperate climate weather that is not too hot or too cold

territory particular area of land that belong to and is controlled by a country

tributary river or stream that flows into larger rivers

vertebrate animal that has a spine, or a backbone

wetland low-lying area, such as a marsh or swamp, where the ground is saturated with water

Find out more

Books

Australia (Countries Around the World), Mary Colson (Heinemann, 2012)

Australia (Discover Countries), Chris Ward (Wayland, 2013)

Australia: Everything You Ever Wanted to Know (Not For Parents), (Lonely Planet, 2013)

Australia (Unpacked), Clive Gifford (Wayland, 2014)

Websites

Find out more about the saltwater crocodiles of Australia at:
http://animals.nationalgeographic.com/animals/reptiles/saltwater-crocodile

Discover more about Australia at:
kids.nationalgeographic.com/content/kids/en_US/explore/countries/australia

Look up facts and statistics about Australia at:
www.bbc.co.uk/news/world-asia-15674351

Play fun games and learn more about Australia's outback at:
pbskids.org/wildkratts/habitats/australian-outback

Index